The Invisible Pastor

A Primer Concerning the Effect of Gnosticism on Ministerial Clothing

By Rev. James DuJack

Printed in the United States of America

First Printing, 2012

ISBN-13: 978-0615673196
ISBN-10: 0615673198

Oakwood Covenant Press
260 Oakwood Avenue
Troy, NY 12182

Scripture Quotations are from The Holy Bible,

King James Version

ACKNOWLEDGEMENT

Even as this work remains timely and important, its recovery is more than a decade old. Lost to time are some source citations. Nevertheless, special thanks and acknowledgement are owed to two in particular, who among many, have certainly influenced my life.

Reflected and presented in this booklet are some of the ideas, insights, and words of wisdom from spiritual mentors: Rev. James B. Jordan in his capacity as an author and an editor and Pastor Doug Wilson. Of course, all errors contained herein are mine alone. While these mentors may or may not have great appreciation for being connected to this work, I have great appreciation for them and their work.

The Invisible Pastor was a sermon delivered to Oakwood Bible Church on July 2nd, 2000.

CONTENTS

Chapter 1: Introduction to Gnosticism

Zechariah 3:1-5 "And HE showed me Joshua the high priest standing before the angel of the LORD, and Satan standing at his right hand to resist him. And the LORD said unto Satan, The LORD rebuke thee, O Satan; even the LORD that hat chosen Jerusalem rebuke thee: is not this a brand plucked out of the fire? Now Joshua was clothed with filthy garments from him. And unto him he said, Behold, I have caused thine iniquity to pass from thee, and I will clothe thee with change of raiment. And I said, Let them set a fair mitre upon his head, and clothed him with garments. And the angel of the LORD stood by".

Today is a day of great celebration for our Church. Three years ago we took a major step forward in our maturation process and becoming mature is a process. Three years ago we began to formalize and focus our Worship Service toward the Biblical Model of Covenant Renewal.

We have greatly matured. Our maturity has been marked by many steps; a proper understanding of The Sacrament of Baptism has been a major one. We also have come to a mature understanding of the Communion Table, so much so that it is now partaken of each week and with wine.

Along the way we have systematically been

weeding out many of the ill effects of **Gnosticism** which is pervasive in our culture and represents a **tendency** at least as much as it represents **heresy.**[1]

I have spoken much, especially this past year about Gnosticism. Gnosticism demotes the importance of the historical aspects of the faith but it also demotes the physical and material aspects and expressions of the faith. *Kneeling is not necessary – we kneel in our hearts. Tithing is not necessary – we tithe in our hearts. Water is not necessary for baptism – it is altogether a "spiritual thing".*

Thankfully this Gnosticism concerning the faith has not spilled over into other spheres of life. Thankfully we are inconsistent, thankfully we are schizophrenic. At least we don't say, *"ah", you don't need any sleep for your physical being, all you need is "spiritual rest".* We don't say, *"you don't need any real food for your body, spiritual nourishment is all you need."* And quite frankly, I don't find too many who practice a "spiritual only" marriage instead of the Biblical one which includes physical intimacy.

Gnosticism also causes us to skew the presentation of the Bible. We think that the Old Testament is solely characterized by things external, temporal, bodily, earthly, visible,

---

[1] For a fuller discussion of this, see Jim Jordan's "Creation in Six Days" pg 71 ff.

objective, and corporate.

Meanwhile we characterize New Testament things as:

> Internal not external
> Eternal not temporal
> Spiritual not bodily
> Heavenly not earthly
> Invisible not visible
> Subjective not objective
> Individual not corporate[2]

Thus we have the curse of our "unreal, irrelevant Christianity". But any clear and fair reading of both Testaments show, that both Testaments posits things as:

> External & internal
> Temporal & eternal
> Bodily & spiritual
> Earthly & heavenly
> Visible & invisible
> Objective & subjective
> Corporate & individual

---

[2] Flinn, P. Richard. "Baptism, Redemptive History, and Eschatology, the Parameters of Debate." *Christianity and Civilization* 1.Spring (1982): 134. Print.

Chapter 2: Clothing

The Bible is like unto a seamless garment. Jesus says the "Scripture cannot be broken" and so, a small piece of Gnosticism causes us to despise physical, material, even **visual things**. A perfect expression of that is, since God only cares about my heart, my clothes don't matter. As a matter of fact, some perversely believe that their casual dress represents an enlightened state of advanced spirituality. And, so we live in the age of the "**First Church of Shorts and Flip-Flops**".[3]

But it is a false reading of Scripture to view the external and visible as unimportant. Revelation 7 shows the Saints in **white robes**. The white baptismal robes of Whitsunday are based on this and the worship in heaven is and is supposed to be a **pattern** for what we do on earth. After all Jesus prayed, "Thy will be done on earth as it is in heaven".

We are told in the Bible, even in the New

---

[33] This is the sort of insightful cultural observation that Rev. Doug Wilson is known for.

Testament that worship includes things; material, physical, audible, and visible; standing, kneeling, trumpets, shouting, seeing.

Now with respect to the Church, we often dismiss the importance of clothing. Thankfully we are inconsistent, even schizophrenic. For we surely and rightfully so, understand and appreciate the importance of clothing in other spheres.

Take for Example, the Wedding Gown: There is no Biblical command; yet no one says, "what makes her think she is so special." Another example is the Graduate Robe: No one says, "who do they think they are, they think they're so smart". The same is true for Judges, Doctors, Policeman, Firemen, and Nurses. These clothes, these uniforms do not **make** them, but they do **mark** them. The Graduation Robe does not add a lick to the IQ of the wearer, it does not **make** them, but it **marks** them for what they have achieved and accomplished. You'd probably also be pretty nervous if your brain surgeon walked into the ER with a tank top, Bermuda shorts, and sneakers.

Marking of these individuals can be very important. A lifeguard at the moment of need is easily identified by his **uniform.** He can be sought out, located easily, and can be called upon and trusted to competently perform a rescue attempt.

Chapter 3: Ministers

Last Saturday, I was out at Burger King with two of my seven sons, Jared and Andrew. Just prior to going out, as I was thinking about that lifeguard illustration, I jotted down its importance. Jared, who has an insatiable interest and thirst for information inquired why I had jotted it down. I explained it all to him, that I wanted to remember it as a good illustration. Anyhow, out at Burger King , before our meal, I bowed in prayer as usual. Upon doing so, a fellow patron stops over and asks, "what church do you belong to"? I told him, and he said "Praise the Lord". Andrew whispers "aren't you going to tell him that you are the Pastor"? I turned to Jared and said, "if I was dressed differently, I wouldn't have to tell him I was the Pastor".

That day, and every day, I, like hundreds of thousands of other ministers, **"I was an Invisible Pastor".** Clothing doesn't **make** the man, but it does **mark** him. Perhaps you've seen the shameful essay about Silent Pastors that Brother Duncan has distributed. This issue, that issue, then the refrain: "and 300,000 pulpits are silent", for sure that silence is shameful.

But you know what, they are also, (for the

most part) **Invisible**. We are horrified at the thought of them being silent, such that our culture fails to hear their protest, yet sound is a sensory; audible, even physical, material phenomenon. Should we not have equal shame that they are not **visible** to the culture, protesting its lawlessness?

As I recall, Pastor Ray Sutton speaks of attending a protest with hundreds of other Pastors. He alone received a hearing with the Governor. Why? For he alone wore a collar. Imagine the godly fear in hearts of magistrates; one hundred collars. What's going on? Do we like our defeat, our weakness, our invisibility? Perhaps it goes hand in hand with our all too often flight from responsibility.

Do you remember the fascinating, arresting photo from Time Magazine during the Rodney King riots? A white truck driver, pulled out by a mob, smashed on his head with a brick and a bottle. The mob circled, a black man rushes in, holding the truck drivers head in his arms. He holds up his hand to the mob which is circling like wolves. His collar is clearly seen. Immediately, like a force field, that mob, those wolves were held back in check. Without that collar, he would be viewed as an Uncle Tom, more likely kicked in the head as well. The clothes did not make him, they **marked** him.

Who   knows   how   many   ministry opportunities are missed when a minister is not

marked and how many times has someone sought **another marked** minister who had not the Gospel but looked like a man where real help could be found.

Chapter 4: Calling

Failure to wear ministerial clothing is another area where the Church has thrown out the baby with the bathwater. The marking of a minister also greatly helps the minister to be continually reminded of his calling in Christ. He is to be a slave. That is one of the meanings of the collar; a servant, a minister, a slave, just as Jesus said in Mark 10:43-44.

"But so shall it not be among you: but whosoever will be great among you, shall be your minister. And whosoever of you will be the chiefest, shall be servant of all."

The collar also acts to remind him of the yoke of his calling. In 1 Corinthians 9; the minister is compared to the oxen treading out the grain, continually giving out the Word, "plowing the fields".

What is a collar? It is a yoke, which is a commitment to the Word. The slave collar, which is a commitment to Christ and His Church. Ministerial clothing in worship also acts to hide the man and exalt the office, instead of the personality cult that so readily defines the Christian culture today.

I will speak more about the Representative Role of the Minister on Wednesday night. God's Covenant requires hierarchy in every sphere. Families have fathers to represent God's authority and Churches have elders. These representatives do not replace but rather they represent Jesus Christ to His people. It is important for you to know that the elders of this Church have required of me to bring forth these teachings on Ministerial clothing.

Did you know that clothing is an inescapable concept? For even going naked would reveal something about ourselves and so the only question really is which clothing? Brethren, ultimately we dress in one of two ways. We dress either **vocationally** or we dress according to what is in **vogue**, you might say status or style. We dress according to our calling under God or according to the fashion of the day, the world, or ourselves. A tie, for example is a symbol of the working business world.

I remember that once, and only once here, my first year, I wore an off white sport coat and white shoes. What did I get? The Pat Boone jokes! People were expecting a rendition of Moon River or something like that. The attention was not on Jesus Christ!

Vocation is something to be proud of, not hidden; it's honorable, it shouldn't be invisible.

Even the calloused hands of the plumber and carpenter are the honorable **marks** of his calling under God. Brethren, I hope we are mature enough to begin to understand and appreciate this.

Chapter 5: Back in Uniform

I believe a great example of all I've talked about today is found in Zechariah 3. I've preached from this passage, even many times about the great symbolism, the great picture of salvation and restoration. It is great spiritual stuff, but that's not all it is, it's not that **gnostic**. It has historical setting, the Babylonian captivity, the temple was destroyed, the priests were stripped, and their outward glory was stripped away under the judgment of God. The priests were not in uniform.

Let's look at Zechariah 3:1-5 again.

Zechariah 3:1-5 "And HE showed me Joshua the high priest standing before the angel of the LORD, and Satan standing at his right hand to resist him. And the LORD said unto Satan, The LORD rebuke thee, O Satan; even the LORD that hath chosen Jerusalem rebuke thee: is not this a brand plucked out of the fire? Now Joshua was clothed with filthy garments from him. And unto him he said, Behold, I have caused thine iniquity to pass from thee, and I will clothe thee with change of raiment. And I said, Let them set a fair mitre upon his head, and clothed him with garments. And the angel of the LORD stood by.

The promise here is that God was going to restore them, not only spiritually, not only inwardly, but visibly and externally. Full restoration took place. The priests were back, gloriously arrayed. This gave the people great hope. Their dominion was to be real in terms of time and history. The filthy, common, unpriestly clothes represented a part of God's negative covenant sanctions, now taken away. This new physical, outward, visible glory was the expression of God's inward, spiritual, invisible favor, His renewed positive Covenant sanction.

The dominion we take, the dominion God gives, is to be accompanied by external, visual expression. It's like "raising a flag" and/or proudly waving a wedding band, and they aren't even Biblically warranted. But horror of horrors, what has happened in American Evangelicalism? Not the enemy, but we ourselves have stripped the ministers and we live in a self-imposed evangelical ghetto, hiding and invisible. We have not taken dominion as commanded.

We don't want our Pastors as Generals. We want them as water boys, perhaps providing aid behind the scenes, out of sight. No victory on the horizon, no leading, no planning, no victory even in sight. No victory even in our theology. We thereby don't need to follow, we can be faithless. Our ministers certainly are not dressed for success before God, our enemies, or the world.

Let me close by saying this, the elders have not only directed and required that I teach on the issue of ministerial clothing, but also that, after the teaching today, that I begin wearing that clothing.

So today, I appeal to you for support and prayer. I will need it. Although I am completely theologically committed to it, the thought unnerves me like few other things. Not at all because I have doubts about it, but I know how it will be received in many circles. Yet I am willing to move forward.

- Some unlearned and arrogant Christians will probably send me "get saved" tracts to try to witness to me.

- I will receive great ridicule from my relatives and acquaintances, Remember, I am a local boy.

- Many Christians will ignorantly view this as a step back into Roman Catholicism. Some will view it as a sign of instability instead of growth and maturity.

- Many Roman Catholics will ridicule me as an imposter.

Where will you fall in that mix? I am committed to move forward regardless of the cost, not the least of which is all of the ridicule. I also know that historically, persecution, the real kind, not gnostic persecution; the real stuff comes on those so visibly marked as their enemies. I am prepared, I trust by the grace of God to be that kind of target. Persecution is coming to the Church of Jesus Christ, even in these United States.

But are you prepared for that for me, and are you mature enough (that's all it is), to embrace this idea? That God's kingdom is to be visibly and externally displayed even as it invisibly and internally grows. The New Testament teaches this extensively as we'll continue to see on Wednesday night.

Pray for me, as I pray for you, as we "come out of diapers", as we come of age and maturity concerning vocational clothing, as we leave behind an **Invisible Pastor**.

The Invisible Pastor